Yorkshire Terriers

Dog Books for Kids

By
K. Bennett

Mendon Cottage Books

JD-Biz Publishing

Read More Amazing Animal Books

Purchase at Amazon.com

Table of Contents

Introduction

My little dog — a heartbeat at my feet.
~Edith Wharton

Yorkshire terriers are beautiful little dogs weighing approximately 7 pounds. They are popular pets and great companions with a "big" personality, despite their size.

They are also vivacious, intelligent, feisty and loving. Although stubborn from time to time, with the right training Yorkie's can be the most adorable pet!

Yorkshire Terriers have an interesting history. This particular breed originated from Northern England, but don't let its size fool you. This little dog packs lots and lots of love. A Terrier's coat is quite beautiful and silky in shades of black, gray or even tan.

When Terriers started out they were used catch rats, but during the Victorian era they became show dogs and beautiful pets. Then after some years passed, people forgot about this small companion… but not for long. When world world II started, something amazing happened. Can you guess what it was?

Yorkie Doodle Dandy appeared… and because of her, everyone fell in love with the terrier all over again. Do you know who Yorkie doodle dandy was? She was a beautiful 4 pound terrier that served during the world war. She was found by an American soldier and for quite some time followed him on combat missions in the pacific, traversed the New Guinea jungle and even an Okinawa typhoon! Her owner, Wynne called her *"An angel from a foxhole."*

This real life story tells you a little about a terrier's personality: *Their protective nature.* This means Yorkie's are not too fond of strangers (or other animals) and they can get a bit aggressive. And if they should see a squirrel, the rest is history as they say.

Yorkie's have a tendency to feed off your emotions. So if you are protective of them and their environment, they will transfer those emotions to their personality and turn into a train wreck! This means they will see danger at every turn, and bark their little life away.

However, the good qualities of Terriers far outweigh the bad ones. For one thing, they love spending time with you. Being underfoot and basking in your warmth and affection is the best gift for a Terrier. So take this aspect of their personality must be considered.

Ultimately, Yorkie's are beautiful and loyal pets with a high degree of intelligence. It may take some time to mold them to family life, but once their love and respect is earned, you will not find a more lovable and charming pet!

Waiting to play

**Chapter 1**

An interesting start – Northern England

As the name indicates, Yorkshire Terriers originated from Yorkshire, England. This is in the Northern part and rugged region of the country. Many years ago, specifically during the 19th century, workers came from Scotland to England for work.

When the workers arrived, they brought different varieties of Terriers. There is not much detail and information on the breeding process of Terriers, but we do know that cotton and woolen mills played a part to develop the breed we know today.

Interestingly, the origin of the Terrier was the combination of three dogs. The male was named Old Crab, the female Kitty and the other name is not known. These dogs were actually Terriers from Scotland, but ended up being called Yorkshire Terriers instead.

In those days, Terriers had a typical long coat, very silky and beautiful. Some said it was the work of the looms of weavers since many Terriers belonged to this group. The dogs boasted splashes of blue with fawn or silver head and legs, trimmed ears and docked tails.

This appearance was generally accepted as a Yorkshire Terrier, but during the latter part of 1860, a dog by the name of Huddersfield Ben was put on display and shocked everyone! Why? He was so beautiful everyone wanted one just like him.

Huddersfield Ben's owner Mary Ann Foster lived in Yorkshire. She entered her pet into many different dog shows and he quickly became a star! He was so well known that George Earl, who knew a lot about Terriers said *"Huddersfield Ben was the best stud dog of his breed during his lifetime, and one of the most remarkable dogs of any pet breed that ever lived; and most of the show specimens of the present day have one or more crosses of his blood in their pedigree."*

Even today, Huddersfield Ben is known as the "Father of the breed," and his descendants defined the Yorkshire terriers making them one of the most beloved pets.

By 1872, Terriers were introduced into North America and the American Kennel Club registered the breed in 1885.

To think about: Terriers tend to forget their size and can be quite courageous. They love adventure and do not always avoid trouble! It can be aggressive towards other dogs and smaller animals. And it can whip up a barking storm if needed! However, you can control your Terrier's impulses with the right training. So before you get a Terrier, weigh the pros and cons of caring for an active and adventurous pet.

Note of advice: Terriers like other breeds thrive on a close relationship. That means you are an inseparable part of the Terriers life. So if you leave your pet alone for long periods of time, they can get down, upset and suffer from anxiety syndrome right down to panic attacks. Having this pet requires responsibility to reassure your pet of your loving attention.

Always here for you

A dog by any other name…

Terriers are not so great with smaller kids. They do better with older children who know how to treat and respect them. But when it comes to adventure they are raring to go! So it is important to take care of this aspect of your dog's nature, and make sure it gets adequate exercise to expend their energy.

Of course the great part about Terriers is their adaptability to apartment living, so with the right daily exercise a Terrier can settled down quite nicely.

A level of adaptability to other animals is also necessary for this pet. If a Terrier is raised with other animals, it adapts quite nicely. However, if you are introducing a new pet to the family, your Terrier may feel differently. They may also look on the new pet as an "intruder" that simply has to go!

This means a fight may be inevitable. And if a fight does break out, your Terrier will not give up. If you love a variety of animals in your home this might be frustrating experience. However, with the right level of socialization and training these reactions can be avoided.

Terriers can be stubborn creatures and training is not easy. If you don't think you can handle this aspect of your dog's personality, there are training and obedience schools that can help. You can also talk to a trusted Veterinarian for their advice.

However, on the upside of this tale, Terriers can whip up a barking storm in a dash! And they can bark loudly and persistently until you feel like pulling your hair out. The breed has been described at *your pure bred puppy* as "keen of eye and sharp of tongue."

Remember: A Terrier's objective is to warn you by any means necessary, so they will do whatever it takes to get your attention. If this quality is too irritating, the Terrier can be trained to keep the barking to a minimum.

Important note: Terriers can be opinionated, stubborn and a bit hard to handle especially when it comes to housebreaking skills. This tiny pet packs a lot of willpower, so it will take time and proper training to ensure a stable and adaptable pet!

Admit it…Don't you think I'm cute?

 **Chapter 2**

Now that you know what Terriers are like and their origins, let us review its features:

In review: Terriers are beautiful little dogs with a lot of courage and skills. They are excellent watchdogs and thrive in a close knit relationship.

Terriers love being underfoot and hate being left alone. To ensure the emotional wellbeing of your pet, remember to spend quality time with them.

When it comes to behavior, a Terrier's enthusiasm and adventurous spirit will bring a smile to your face and leave you wanting for more.

They are even friendly with other animals once they are properly socialized. As a whole, Terriers are "small" dogs with "larger than life" personalities.

Would you like to get one?

A quick word of advice: A Terrier can take over if you are not careful. They may impose their own will and teach "*you*" how "*they*" should be treated and not the other way around. To curb this behavior, TRAIN your Terrier to follow your commands from the beginning. Also teach them what kind of behavior is acceptable and what kind of behavior is not allowed!

FUN FACTS FOR KIDS: Terriers are very intelligent dogs. On the list of intelligence according to Stanley Coren, Terriers are ranked in the 27th range. Do you know what this means? Ask a parent or guardian to help you search online to see how many repetitions it takes before a Terrier obeys!

So happy here!

- How much can they weigh? The male and female can weigh approximately 7 pounds. This doesn't mean a Terrier can't weigh more / less than this, but this is the standard weight.

-How tall can they get? Terriers can reach 6 - 9 inches in height.

-What about babies? Terrier's litters vary. The female can have between 1 -7 puppies. However, the average size is 3 - 4 puppies.

-How long to they live? Lifespan is usually between 10 - 15 years.

-What about their coat? Terriers typically have a long, beautiful, silky coat. If their coat is very long, you need to brush regularly.

-How often do they shed? Terriers are not great shedders and shed lightly if at all. If you suffer from allergies, this pet may be perfect for you!

-What color are they? Terriers have beautiful coats in lustrous shades of black, dark gray and tan. But this is not the only color of the Terriers coat. This variety extends to silver, blue, light brown and creamy tones!

- What about their temperament or personality? As noted previously, Terriers have a defined personality. And their high intelligence and loyalty are delightful aspects of their nature. However, they are not too fond of young children, and can easily get out of hand with their overprotective skills. Proper socialization in Terriers is extremely important for a well-rounded pet.

A moment of peace and tranquility

Caring for your Terrier

Terriers are not only our pets, but also valued members of our home. So we want to be sure they get proper care and like most, if not all of us, the right diet and exercise is important.

*** *It is important to note Terriers do not overeat like other dog breeds, so you can let your pet "free feed." This means you do not need to regulate the portions of food, but let your pet decide when to eat and how much to eat.*

As a general rule you may want to know…how you can be sure if your pet is being fed correctly. The same principle applies for other breeds, but this general rule of thumb is a nice way to test your animal to see how well they are eating.

Try the following test listed on **dogtime.com** at home. Are you ready?

FIRST: Put your thumbs on his spine and run your fingers along the side of the Terrier's body.

SECOND: Once there, feel for his ribs beneath the muscle. If you can see them, he needs more food or a nutritional supplement!

In a Terriers case due to his small size, just looking at your pet will give you an indication of how well your meal plan is going.

A snack right now would be good :-)

Mealtime

There are lots of choices to feed your Terriers, so it may be hard to choose the best food on the market. These steps (below) will help you make an informed and honest decision regarding the best dog food for your beloved pet. (This advice applies to other breeds as well).

Grrmf.org notes the following recommendations to ensure a happy and healthy pet.

Scratch chemical preservatives: Be on the lookout for ingredients like Ethoxyquin, BHT, BHA, propelyne glycol or sodium nitrates in any form. That includes sodium nitrites too! Instead look for natural preservatives such as Rosemary (herbs), and natural Tocopherols.

Expiration date: Be sure to check the expiration date on the bag. You should purchase food months ahead of this date. Why? Moldy food could be a health factor and you never want to feed your dog this kind of food, which can affect its good health. Usually the bag itself is an indicator. Does it look fresh or do you see grease stains somewhere?

Stay away from those unsavory looking bags! Ask the store helpers if you are not sure whether the bag is fresh or not.

A bite of meat: Meat ingredient is a great choice, but be sure it is the FIRST ingredient. This can be Turkey, Lamb or Chicken. Do not buy food with Grain as the first ingredient. Why not? Meat protein is what you are looking for. This is the best nutrition for your pet so search for the meat ingredient as one of the most (if not the most) important in the list. Remember your pet needs animal protein for a beneficial diet.

Avoid animal digest: This is the intestines of other animals! They can contain feet, heads and slaughterhouse waste of other animals. An example as noted at the website is "poultry byproducts."

Sugars and artificial colors: These additives are not healthy or beneficial for your pet so avoid them.

Dog treats: Try to get healthy treats! There are many out there with ingredients that could harm your pet. You could try your hand at making them yourself. Make it family project and have some fun.

The list could go on and on, but you get the idea! Of course if you have the time to make home cooked food for your pet it would be a great alternative to ensure healthy meals.

The website **Yorkieinfocenter.com** noted some great tips to help you give the best nutrition to your pet. It also lists the quantities and portions of meals if you would like to do a meal plan.

The recommended meat ingredients among others are:

White chicken meat - broiled
Hamburger - lean
Fish
Kidney
Liver

Next are the vegetables. (Mixture of two is recommended)

Green beans – cut up

Carrots – cut up
Sweet peas
Sweet potatoes
Beets

A helping of starch:

Brown or white rice
Pasta

Finish off with an excellent multivitamin or supplement (for dogs) and voila! A well fed, healthy and happy pet.

Note: Not all of us have time to do home cooked meals for our pets, and your pet may not be a fan of vegetables! However, if you decide to purchase commercial dog food, take the time to find the healthiest alternative available and the most nutritious supplements for your pet.

Caution: We all know what foods **NOT** to feed our dogs. You may instantly think of chocolate. But you can add to this list: mushrooms, caffeine, onions, fruit seeds, grapes, raisins and more. If you are unsure of the entire list, look online to see what other foods you need to avoid. And if you are underage, please consult with a parent or guardian before you start your search.

Exercises

Terriers require daily exercise and this can include:

-Breaking a little sweat

Terriers need exercise. So you can jog, run or walk to get their blood flowing. (Note: This is a daily requirement, so if you unable to meet this type of demand on your time, a Terrier may not be the ideal pet for you – If you still want one but need to find other ways to keep the pet happily occupied, talk to a dog trainer or reputable veterinarian for their advice.)

-Soft run

One of the best ways to keep your Terrier happy is by stretching your legs into a soft run. (Not too fast…remember your pet is a small dog with little feet) And try to stay away from really hard surfaces. An open field (park area or similar site) is better for its low impact on the frame of your pet. This will help their joints and feet to keep in tip top shape.

- Indoor activities

Terriers are also active indoors and this helps them to expend energy. This is a great help for your exercise routine, since you will not have to expend a great deal of energy outdoors to ensure your pet gets adequate exercise.

Making friends

Living with the family

Children and Terriers have an interesting relationship, and some of it is not too great. As we have learned, to interact with family pets (Like other dogs and cats), there is a degree of socialization required for Terriers. This applies to young children as well.

In the case of Terriers this will take time, patience and lots of loving attention. Although they are easy to train sometimes, in other areas this training can be difficult. An example is housebreaking rules.

Terriers will simply "go" wherever they want to! So if you do not want an unpleasant surprise, you must train your pet to "go" where you want him to go. It should be noted that this is much easier said than done with this breed.

So how will you handle it? *Your pure bred puppy* recommends the following two important steps:

1 – **CONFINEMENT**: Let you pet know he / she will not be allowed to roam around the house UNTIL they are properly trained. This area

should be sectioned off and your pet must remain in there at all times. This may be difficult at first. You may feel your pet is too confined and should roam freely. Please remember that he / she will be free! This measure is only temporary. Once your pet learns the right skill, they can roam as much as they like.

Why is this necessary? If you do not START the training in the right way, and a bad habit takes over...it will be almost impossible to break! So take this aspect of your Terrier's behavior into consideration and decide what kind of pet you would prefer.

2- REGULAR / CONSTANT ACCESS TO THE "GO" AREA:
Your pet needs access to the "go" area at all times. Once he / she is properly housebroken, do not change the rules and change the "go" area. That way your pet will automatically return to the area when needed.

Two simple steps to try. Of course there are other things we can do, but this is a great way to start. If you would like to more details check online, or talk to a reputable veterinarian or dog trainer.

🐾 Chapter 3

You know we look good!

So, what else can we learn about Terriers? Check out some other details you may like to know.

- Terriers do not really shred. So if you are allergic or prone to allergies this might be an ideal dog for you.

- Terriers usually have a lot of hair, so you still need to brush them regularly. If you don't, their hair can tangle or get matted and that will make your little terrier very unhappy.

- Your little Terrier is fragile so be careful. They can get bone problems, teeth problems and even indigestion. So be careful when you move or play with them. If you are careful, both you and your Yorkie will enjoy many years of happy times together.

- Terriers have keen senses and make excellent watchdogs. If a stranger approaches you will be the first to know!

- A Yorkie may need to get his / her nails trimmed from time to time. A good way to know if the nails are too long is to listen to their feet. If you hear clicking sounds every time your Terrier walks….the nails are too long and need a trim!

- A cold environment is not for a Terrier. They simply hate it to death! Why? They are easy to get chilled or much too cold for their comfort.

Twice the fun

FUN FACTS FOR KIDS: Have you heard of ***Sylvia the matchbox Terrier***? She was owned by Arthur Maples of Blackburn, England. Would you like to know what made her unique? Check it out online, but be sure to ask for permission first!

Conclusion

Bonding time

In conclusion:

Terriers can be adorable lapdogs and a great family pet. Of course, they can be stubborn and independent, but they are also tons of fun if properly socialized!

If needed, Terriers can get quite loud and overprotective. And when it comes to strangers, they bark first and ask questions later. So if you need an excellent watchdog with keen instincts, this little dog may be perfect for you!

They can also be stubborn, opinionated and neurotic from time to time. But their loyalty and energetic nature outshines most flaws. When proper boundaries are established, a Yorkie will thrive in a loving home. And as the years go by, they will become an intricate part of your family life.

If you decide to make this breed a part of your family home, you could not make a more interesting choice than a feisty and lovable pet!

Author Bio

K. Bennett is a native from the Island of Roatan, North of Honduras. She loves to write about many different subjects, but writing for children is special to her heart.

Some of her favorite pastimes are reading, traveling and discovering new things. These activities help to fuel her imagination and act like a canvas for more stories.

She also loves fantasy elements like hidden worlds and faraway lands. Basically anything that gets her imagination soaring to new heights!

Her writing credits include local newspaper articles, a writing blog at Wordpress.com and other online stories. It also includes nonfiction books, children books online, and two novellas listed at Amazon.com

Our books are available at

1. Amazon.com

2. Barnes and Noble

3. Itunes

4. Kobo

5. Smashwords

6. Google Play Books

This book is published by

JD-Biz Corp

P O Box 374

Mendon, Utah 84325

http://www.jd-biz.com/

Made in the USA
Middletown, DE
03 May 2019